<u>Prefa</u>

What do you do when football

Mass?

Jack, a seven year old who has just started in Year 3 at a new school, has to make a decision about whether to give up Sunday football club in order to go to Mass on Sunday. At age seven, he is old enough to go to Mass every week, and he is about to start First Holy Communion classes. But in this story, he learns that some things in life are more important even than football...

A Catholic story, suitable for children of all ages, but particularly for those of around seven years who are preparing for First Holy Communion.

Suitable for parents to read to children, for catechists to use as a discussion point, and with simple enough language for children to read themselves.

Children will learn that Mass is very special - the bread and wine become Jesus' Body, Blood, Soul and Divinity, and that the Church teaches that Catholics must go to Mass on Sundays and holy days of obligation.

Catholic Stories for Children: Sunday Football

(My First Holy Communion Book 1)

ANNE JOACHIM

ACKNOWLEDGMENTS

Saints Anne and Joachim, Jesus' grandparents, pray for us!

FOOTBALL CLUB

Jack's new house had a long garden.

"Perfect for football!" he shouted joyfully to his Mum and Dad on the day they moved in. His parents smiled. They had been so busy over the summer holidays getting everything ready for the move, that they hadn't had much time to spend with Jack. They hadn't even had time to show him the new house before they decided to buy it.

"Thank goodness he likes football," said Dad. "It will be easy for him to make friends at his new school, because lots of children like football."

But when Jack started at the new school, he had a surprise. At assembly on the first day, the head of school stood up and told the children that football was banned.

"Last term, we had too many children getting hurt during football matches," she said. "So from now on, no ball games will be allowed in the playground. You will have to find other games to play."

Lots of the children complained, but Jack was quiet. Since he was new, he didn't know the other children very well yet, and he didn't want to get into trouble on his first day.

"Stand up, Year 3," said his teacher, and Jack remembered to stand up with the rest of his new class. He followed them quietly down the corridor to his new classroom.

When they got into the classroom, Jack sat down on the carpet with the other children.

"My name is Mrs Blakey," said the teacher. "Some of you know me already, but there are also some new children in the class, so I am going to sit each of the new children next to a special friend who will look after you."

Mrs Blakey talked to the children about how they could make the new children feel welcome. A boy called Toby put his hand up a lot, and had lots of ideas.

"We could help them if they look lost," he said. "And we could play with them at break time."

Jack was happy when Mrs Blakey told him Toby would be his special friend and so they would sit next to each other.

"Do you like football?" Jack asked Toby as soon as they sat at their table.

"It's OK," said Toby.

But another boy sitting at the same table had overheard and leaned over to say, "I LOVE football! It's so unfair that we can't play football at school!"

"I don't care," said another boy, who was called Sam. "I go to football club at Ropers' at the weekend so I get to play football every week. And because we've started back at school on a Friday, it's the weekend tomorrow, so I don't care."

Just then, Mrs Blakey asked the class to be quiet, so Jack couldn't ask Sam any more about the football club.

When the school day was over, Jack's Dad came and collected him from school.

"Did you have a good day?" asked Dad.

"Can I go to football club?" said Jack immediately. He had ignored his Dad's question because he was so excited that he wasn't really listening.

"I don't know," replied Dad. "But you should say,

'please can I go to football club?'."

"PLEASE can I go to football club?"

"I don't know," said Dad again. "But as it's the weekend, we can play football in our new garden."

When they got home, Mum wanted to know all about Jack's first day at his new school. But all he said was,

"It was OK. But I wish I could go to football club."

That night, when Mum and Jack were saying their bedtime prayers, Jack prayed,

"God bless Mummy, God bless Daddy, God bless me and please God can I go to football club."

Now, Mum and Dad really cared about Jack. They wanted him to be happy in their new house and the new school. And they wanted to promise Jack that he could go to football club, because they thought he would enjoy it and might make some new friends. But they couldn't promise this yet because they didn't know whether there were any spaces left, or how much it would cost.

When Jack had gone to bed, his parents had a long talk.

"Do you think Jack had a good day at school?" asked Mum.

"I don't know. He didn't talk much about how school was."

"I wish he could have told me more about his day. All he would say was, "It's OK." I don't feel I learned much about what happened at school."

"And he kept saying he wanted to join the football club."

"Yes, do you know if there is a football club around here? Perhaps you could google it?"

"I don't need to," said Dad. "I already spoke to one of the other parents and they told me there is a football club every Sunday morning. It's called "Roper's". Lots of Jack's new class go to it, including a boy called Sam who sits on his table. It's too late for Jack to go to Ropers this weekend, but we can book him in to start the Sunday after."

"But what time is it?" asked Mum. "Remember that Mass is at 11 o' clock on Sunday."

"It's at 11 o' clock too, but that's OK," said Dad, who

wasn't a Catholic and didn't go to Mass. "I'll take him, so you can still go to Mass."

Mum was worried. Dad didn't understand that Jack was now old enough to go to Mass every Sunday.

"But Jack will need to go to Mass, too."

"He doesn't need to," said Dad. "He's still a child. He can go to football club instead."

"He's seven now," said Mum. "Seven is the age when he is supposed to do his First Holy Communion. He needs to go to Mass every Sunday."

Mum and Dad both felt sad because they didn't agree about Jack going to Mass on Sunday. Dad couldn't understand why it was important, and Mum felt sorry because she knew it was important, but she also wanted Jack to be able to go to football club.

"Well, I'll call them up on Monday and see if there is any space left to start next week," said Dad. "Then we can decide what happens after that."

The next day, Mum, Dad and Jack all played football together in the garden. Jack had a brilliant time.

"Can we do this tomorrow, too, after Mass?" he

asked.

"Yes, of course," said Mum. "In fact, there's a park right next to the church, so we could bring the football with us and play there."

"I wish I could go to football club," said Jack. He didn't mean to be rude, but he found he couldn't help keep complaining about it, even though he knew his parents would do what was best for him. "Anyway, Mass doesn't start until 11am, so why don't we go to the park before Mass?"

"That should be fine," said Mum.

Early on Sunday morning, Jack and Mum went to the park next to the church. There was nobody else there, so they kicked the football around.

"This is great!" said Jack. Mum smiled.

Just before it was time to go to Mass, people began arriving in the park. Jack recognised Toby from school. Toby was with his little brother, Zac.

"Hello, Toby!"

"Hello!" said Toby. "Are you here for football club?"

Jack's face fell.

"No," he said. "I'm just playing football with my Mum before I go to Mass at that church over there."

"Why do you go to Mass?" asked Toby.

Jack felt silly because he didn't know how to answer Toby's question. His Mum had taken him to Mass lots of times, but he couldn't remember ever thinking about why they went.

"I'll tell you on Monday," he said quickly. "I've got to go. My Mum's waiting."

Jack ran across the field to where his Mum was waiting for him.

"Who was that?" asked Mum.

"Toby," said Jack. "Mum, why is it that we go to Mass?"

"We go because Jesus asked us to," Mum replied. "The night before Jesus died, he had supper with his disciples."

"I know, the Last Supper," added Jack. "His disciples were his friends."

"That's right. And they were more than just friends.

They followed him and believed in him. They believed that Jesus really was God, and they trusted that what he said was true. And at the Last Supper, Jesus broke some bread and gave it to his disciples. He said, "Take this, all of you, and eat of it, for this is my Body, which will be given up for you.""

"I know that," said Jack. "But why do we have to go to Mass?"

"Well, then Jesus took some wine and he said, "Take this, all of you, and drink from it, for this is the chalice of my Blood, the Blood of the new and eternal covenant, which will be poured out for you and for many for the forgiveness of sins.""

"Yes, I know that too," said Jack. "But that still doesn't answer the question of why we have to go to Mass."

"Well, when Jesus said those words over the bread, and over the wine, they truly became his Body and Blood, Soul and Divinity. That's exactly what happens at Mass. The priest says the words of Jesus, and the bread and wine really become Jesus' Body, Blood, Soul and

Divinity. When people go up to the front to receive Holy Communion, they are not receiving bread, but they are actually receiving Jesus' own Body, Blood, Soul and Divinity. And the reason the priest celebrates Mass, and we come to Mass, is that after Jesus had said all those things, he added, "Do this in memory of me." So that was a command for us to celebrate Mass, in memory of him."

Jack nodded. He thought he understood it a bit better now that he realised Jesus had said, "Do this in memory of me". Jack and Mum went to Mass together.

Half way through the Mass, when the priest held up the bread and repeated Jesus' words from the Last Supper, Jack noticed that his Mum bowed her head very low. Jack thought about what Mum had said.

"Wow," he thought. "So now, that is really Jesus. It isn't bread anymore. That's amazing!"

At the end of Mass, the priest asked everyone to sit down because he wanted to tell them something.

"I have some very good news!" he began. "We are

starting our classes for First Confession and First Holy Communion next week. If there is any child who is in Year 3 or above who would like to prepare for receiving Jesus at Mass – that is, who would like to receive Holy Communion – then please let me know. Classes will be on a Saturday morning."

As Mum and Jack left the church, Jack tugged at his mother's sleeve.

"I'm in Year 3," he said. "Can I go to the Holy Communion classes?"

The priest was waiting at the door and overheard Jack.

"I haven't met you before," said the priest. "Are you new to the parish?"

"Yes," said Jack's Mum. "We moved into our new house last week. My name is Marion, and this is my son, Jack."

"Welcome to St Michael's, Marion and Jack! I'm Father John. Jack, did I hear you say you would like to receive Jesus in Holy Communion?" asked Father John, turning to Jack.

"Yes, please!" said Jack.

"Well then, you will need to come to Mass every Sunday, and to the special classes every Saturday."

"That's a lot," said Jack. "I like to play football on Saturday. I'm not sure I'll have time to go to the classes."

"And his Dad wants him to go to football club on Sunday," added Mum, sadly.

"Football club!" repeated Jack, who didn't know that his Mum and Dad had been talking about it. "Wow! I can't wait! I REALLY want to go to football club! I'm going to football club!"

The priest smiled.

"Perhaps you had better wait another year then before you receive Jesus."

"What do you mean?" asked Jack. "Why do I have to wait? I thought you said it was open to Year 3 children and I've just started in Year 3."

"Have you now?" smiled the priest. "But even so, only children who really understand that Holy Communion is special can make their First Holy

Communion. Little children don't receive Holy Communion because sometimes they don't understand that the bread and wine really become Jesus. They think that they are still bread and wine."

"But I'm not like that," said Jack. "I know that Mass is the same as the Last Supper, and the bread and wine really become Jesus' Body, Blood, Soul and Divinity, just like Jesus said."

Mum looked at Jack proudly. He had said all those big words very carefully and got them right.

"But if you understand that," said the priest. "Don't you want to receive Jesus more than doing anything else? Don't you want to receive Jesus more than going to football club?"

Jack paused.

"Well, yes and no. You see, yes I do want to receive Jesus. But I also want to go to football club. What I don't understand is why I can't go to Mass on another day and receive Jesus. Why do I have to go on Sunday? Couldn't I go to Mass on say a Monday instead? Then I could go to football club on Sunday as well!"

"There are lots of answers to that question," said the priest. "And if you come to our classes, you will learn all about Jesus and what we need to do to prepare for First Confession and First Holy Communion. But if you have time now, we can go into the parish hall where they are having tea and biscuits, and we can sit down and talk about all your questions."

Jack looked at Mum. She nodded, as if it was OK. Jack looked across the road at the park and saw that Toby was still in the field playing football. If he went over now, he might be able to join in.

But then Jack did something really good. He chose to stay and listen to the priest, even though he wanted to play football instead.

"OK," he said. "Thank you."

They went and sat down together in the parish hall. An old lady brought a plate of biscuits and offered them to Jack. Jack looked uncertainly at the priest, and then took a big chocolate one when the priest nodded. The lady brought Mum and the priest a cup of tea, and brought Jack some juice.

"Do you know why Sunday is a special day?" asked the priest, once everyone had a biscuit and a drink.

"Because you don't have to go to school?" guessed Jack.

"In some countries, you do have to go to school on a Sunday," said the priest. "But why do you think you don't have to go to school on Sunday here, in a Christian country?"

Suddenly, Jack remembered something his Mum had told him before.

"Isn't it because Sunday is a day of rest?"

"That's right," smiled the priest. Mum looked proud again. "After God created the world, on the seventh day, God finished his work and God rested on this day and made it holy and blessed it. God's people, the Jewish people, respected this and always observed a Sabbath rest on a Saturday. The world was created for the worship and adoration of God. The Jewish people adored and worshipped God on the Sabbath, and made sure that they didn't do any work which might get in the way of their worship of God."

"So I can go to Mass on Saturday, then!" said Jack triumphantly. "Then I can go to football club on Sunday!"

"Well," smiled the priest. "I was talking about the Jewish Sabbath. But for us, a new day has dawned. When Jesus came and dwelt among us two thousand years ago, he observed the Sabbath on a Saturday. But after he died and rose again from the dead on Easter Sunday, the work of creation was surpassed by the splendour of the new creation at Jesus' resurrection. So because Jesus rose from the dead on a Sunday, Christians now celebrate the Sabbath on a Sunday."

"So Sunday is very special," said Jack. "I see that."

"Yes, and when Catholics all go to Mass on a Sunday, it is a sign to everyone of God's goodness. Outward, visible, public and regular worship helps other people understand that we are united in our love and worship of God. Not only that, but also it helps us. Let me give you an example. Does your Mum make sure you eat properly every day?"

"Yes," nodded Jack. "She makes sure I have healthy

food and I have to eat at least one good meal a day."

"Why does she do that?"

"Because it's healthy and good for me. If I didn't eat properly, I would be ill."

"That makes sense. Your Mum makes that a rule that you eat healthily because she loves you and wants you to be well. Well, think about it like this. The Catholic Church is like your Mum, except the Church is the mother of all of us. She also wants to make sure that we stay healthy and do things which are good for us. She especially looks after our spiritual needs. She knows that we need regular healthy spiritual food. So, she requires that we go to Mass regularly. She knows that if we didn't have to go to Mass on Sundays, then we probably would find other things in life getting in the way (like football club!). So she says that we must go to Mass on Sundays and other holy days of obligation. That can be on the holy day itself, or the evening before. Of course, going to Mass is wonderful, so it isn't really that tough. We just need to understand what's happening, and then we can really start to enjoy going to Mass."

"So will the First Holy Communion classes help me understand what's happening at Mass?"

"They should do," said the priest. "And you can spend your whole life getting to know Jesus better and understanding what's happening at Mass, and learning to enjoy loving Jesus more. You know you can go to Mass on any day, but the only days you have to go to Mass are on Sundays and holy days of obligation when we are celebrating something really important that we need to know about. Like Christmas!"

"Do lots of people go to Mass on days when they don't have to, like Mondays?" asked Jack curiously.

"Some people do," said the priest. "But not as many because people go to work and school and things on those days. That's another reason why it is so good to have the rule that we go to Mass on Sunday. It helps when we have people gathering together to strengthen one another under the guidance of the Holy Spirit. The Church is kind and tries to make it easy for us to fulfil our obligation. So you can go to Mass the evening before a Sunday or holy day of obligation. But because I also say Mass at parishes on the other side of town, we don't have a Saturday evening Mass at this church. Anyway, I can see you are getting tired," said the priest. "And you will need to have your lunch soon, if you are going to eat healthily! It was lovely to meet you. I hope to see you again soon. And," he winked at Jack. "I will pray to the Holy Spirit that you make the right decision about whether to make your First Holy Communion this year."

Jack and Mum thanked the priest and said goodbye.

By the time they got back to the park, Toby was gone. The park was empty again.

"You did really well speaking to that priest, Jack," said Mum after they had kicked the ball around for a while. "I was very proud of you."

Jack smiled. He liked to make his Mum proud.

"Is it true that Dad wants me to go to football club?" he asked.

"Yes," said Mum. "We both want you to go. I just wish it was at another time. This is only a small church so there is only one Mass on a Sunday, which means that football club and Mass both happen at the same time.   Unfortunately, you can't do both, and unfortunately the other parish where Father John says Saturday evening Mass is just too far away for us to get to and then back again in time for your bedtime."

For a while, Jack kicked the ball to his Mum in silence. He was battling in his mind about what decision he should make. Mum was silent, too. She was thinking about how the priest had promised to pray to the Holy Spirit that Jack would make the right decision. Had she known it, the Holy Spirit was already at work.

"Mum," said Jack, suddenly. "I think I've decided about football club."

Mum had been picking up the rucksack with their lunchtime sandwiches in it. She stopped to listen to Jack.

"What have you decided?"

"I want to go to football club. But I don't want it so much as to miss receiving Jesus in Holy Communion. I'm old enough now to start thinking about things like that, and I do understand the special things that happen at

Mass. I want to get to understand that better. So I'm sorry to disappoint Daddy and maybe you, but I won't go to football club. I want to go to Mass instead."

Mum was so happy and surprised that she dropped the rucksack, and their sandwiches rolled all over the muddy ground. She didn't mind at all, and ran forwards to hug Jack.

Jack laughed. He hadn't realised that it had meant so much to Mum.

"Oh dear," he laughed. "We don't have any sandwiches now!"

"Never mind," said Mum, who was laughing too. "There's a café next to the church. Let's have a special treat and eat lunch there."

When they went into the café, lo and behold, Toby was there with his little brother and his Mum!

"Hello, Toby!" said Jack. "This is my Mum. Mum, this is Toby. He's in my class at school."

Toby also introduced Jack to his own Mum and his brother, Zac.

"I'm Jack's special friend at school," Toby said to his

Mum. "That means I am looking after him to make sure he is happy and settles in."

Jack's Mum and Toby's Mum started talking to each other.

"Did you enjoy your football club?" Jack asked Toby.

"What do you mean?" asked Toby. "That wasn't my football club. That was my little brother, Zac's, football club."

"Oh, so it isn't the one that Sam goes to, then?" asked Jack. Sam was the boy who had first mentioned football club at school.

"Oh no," said Toby. "Sam doesn't live near here. The football club he goes to is Ropers. It's a 20 minute drive down the road. My Mum takes us to this one because it's so close to home. Zac's club is at 11, and then we have lunch here, and then my football club starts at 12.45. I tell you what, Jack, you should come. They always like to have new people!"

Jack stopped still in his tracks. He turned to his Mum, who was still speaking to Toby's Mum. And he laughed when he realised they had been talking about exactly the same thing, as Toby's Mum exclaimed exactly at that moment,

"Jack should come. They always like to have new people!"

Jack's Mum turned to him and smiled.

"So you will be able to go to football club, after Mass! You can go to the same football club that Toby goes to. Dad will be pleased!"

And he was. Dad came to watch Jack at football club every Sunday afternoon. Sometimes he also joined Mum and Jack at Mass beforehand. Like on the day when, a few months later, Jack made his First Holy Communion. Mum and Dad were both very proud of him.

"Do you know, Mum," said Jack when they were going home on the day of his First Holy Communion. "If you hadn't dropped those sandwiches that day, and taken me to the café for lunch, we might never have found out about the football club in the park next to the church."

"And if you hadn't decided that going to Mass was more important than football, then you wouldn't have received Jesus today!"

Jack smiled. Since he had been going to First Holy Communion classes, he now knew a lot more about God and understood Mass a lot better. And he knew that the Holy Spirit really had been at work. He knew that sometimes God asks something of us which is difficult, but when we say "yes", there is always a greater happiness than when we say "no". This time, Jack had been able to go to football club as well as receiving his First Holy Communion, but he knew that sometimes we might truly have to give up something we want in order to do what God wants us to do.

This knowledge helped Jack through his whole life, and he always tried to do the right thing... even when it meant missing football!

Dear Jesus, please help us all to try to do the right thing, even when it means giving up something that we want. Amen.

☐ <u>Would you and your parents like to find out more about Jesus and the Catholic Church which he founded?</u>

God has revealed himself to us throughout the ages, and speaks to us through Scripture in the Bible. You will probably be able to get a copy of the Bible at the library, online, or at school. A good starting point is the New Testament, which talks about what Jesus did on earth and includes the story of the Last Supper.

The Catechism of the Catholic Church is a treasure trove of information about what the Catholic Church teaches. Use the index at the back to look up the answers to any questions you have.

Jesus remains present in the Catholic Church. After Mass, the Host, which used to be bread but which is now Jesus' Body, Blood, Soul and Divinity, is usually placed carefully into a little box called a tabernacle. A candle is lit by the tabernacle so that you know that Jesus is there. You can go to a Catholic church and find Jesus waiting for you there, waiting for you to pray to him. You can also go to Mass at a Catholic church. This might also be a good way to meet a Catholic priest, and you can ask him questions about God and religion.

May the Holy Spirit help you make all the right decisions. Amen.

Catholic Stories for Children: Sunday Football

(My First Holy Communion Book 1)

by Anne Joachim

Look out for more Catholic stories in this series, available on Amazon.

Printed in Great Britain
by Amazon